BALLET MADONNAS

Poems by
Lyn Lifshin

Shoe Music Press

Ballet Class Madonna

keeps her
upper body
separate from
what's below
it like the
Victorians

Off Men Ballet Madonna

splits but
not for one of
them her sweat's
from what she
does on her own
twisting, in
control there's
nothing that
can hurt her
except her
toes

Madonna Who Cares Too Much To Do Well In Ballet, With Men

pushes herself
until she's sore

Hooked On Ballet Madonna

becomes as narrow
as her chest

Madonna Who Puts Too Much Into Dance

tho it demands
more than she
has like certain
lovers leaves
her bruised and
sore frustrated
like someone
fused by abuse
who keeps think-
ing if she just
tried harder
it could be as
good as she
imagines

Ballet Madonnas

jerky but
with grace
like little
puppets the
string runs from
something in-
visible down
thru their
brains where
what was wild
is controlled,
bound as a
Chinese woman's
stunted foot
or words,
like their
own toes
crammed to
blood in a
coffin of
a pointe shoe

New Pointe Shoes Madonna

each toe feels
like someone with
its own house
suddenly crammed
together in an
apartment

Ballet Madonna

can balance
where it seems
no one should.
Her legs could
chop down a
door but her
arms are weak,
can't hold you

Madonna Told Screwing Is Very Good For Ballet Turnout

vows to turn
on more to
be turned on to
turnout more
no matter how
it turns out

Pirouette Madonna

isn't as easy
as she seems,
makes you dizzy

Waiting Madonna

is like the stage
before a ballet when
all the seats are
empty dark and
unmagical longing
for toes and hands

Performance Madonna

is like a dancer
who does what's
expected even if
she's not in
the mood she'd
rather be firm
than formed by
what others
lust for she's
on wears clean
clothes her
lips glow are
sucking you the
mirror you see
yourself in the
way you want

Madonna Of The Poems

like lambs wool
stuffed in a pointe
slipper wrapped
around toes that
need something
to nest in some-
thing to keep
where hard
wood slams
what holds you
up touches a
cushion that soaks
up blood takes
on your shape

New Pointe Shoes Madonna

each foot feels
trapped as an
insomniac under
a ceiling of
clocks trying
to do what she
has to as what
holds her
closes in

Madonna's Dream Of The Performance

someone's spilled
talcum all over
their sweat turned
the floor slippery
the mirror pulls
like sea off Big
Sur making cars
fall thru slopes
of iceplant. Her
leotard tears
like silk soaked
in Clorox, some-
thing pounds in
her like a siren
no one can shut
off going off
by mistake until
in tulle with
light perfect,
she's transformed,
a swimmer plunging
into a sea of faces

Madonna Who Puts Too Much Into Dance

tho she comes out of
it bruised and shaking
as someone with a lover
who beats her up, is
always pushing her farther
her bones ache she's
on her knees breaking
thinks if she could just
do it right she'd
have it all

Madonna Who Puts Too Much Into Ballet

like someone joining
a cult who puts on
blinders hardly
eats or sleeps is in
a daze bending into
odd positions doesn't
call old friends
doesn't phone her
mother is too
tired at night to
dream, forgets
who she was

Madonna Who Puts Too Much Into Dance

spreads her legs
every night for
what makes her
ache leaves
her sore as a
man who just
wants a night
on the floor in
a black g string
doing it in 17
positions till
falling home
drained she
feels she's
just her body,
would be alone
if it doesn't
hold up

Turnout Madonna

turns out at the
barre not to
mention sheets
of paper and linen
turns men chewing
clove gum out
reads for a big
turnout burns
as she turns
you on then
out

Ballet Madonna

muscles tight
as a fist
seal her together
stretching at
the barre opening
in a sweat that
cools her body
the way no
man could

Ballet Madonna

circles of light
beamed on arches

swallows in the rigging
violins flutes people

waving programs as fans
Even the grand piano

seems to be sweating

Madonna Of The Abandonments

turns, hearing
his voice now just
on the air, is
that pale pointe
shoe flung maybe
or lost maybe
even longed for
missed as that
pink freezing to
grey snow on Barrett
St, ribbon
strangely haunting
as Ophelia's
hair in the water

Madonna Who Was Nearly Married To
Six Nights A Week Of Ballet

opening and bending
sweating and stretching
so hard she just
flopped down later
on the bed not
caring about phones
or dinner no man
to love or lose sleep
over tho she might
mourn her lost
arabesque how her
back betrayed her
She stopped going out
to films talking
on the phone until
people said addicted
and so she left that
barre for a bar
only to find her
self opening and
sweaty for strangers
who want her to

bend backwards,
be more flexible
and not even feel
good afterward

About the Author

Lyn Lifshin's ANOTHER WOMAN WHO LOOKS LIKE ME was published by Black Sparrow at David Godine October, 2006. It has been selected for the 2007 Paterson Award for Literary Excellence for previous finalists of the Paterson Poetry Prize. (ORDER@GODINE.COM). Also out in 2006, her prize winning book about the famous, short lived beautiful race horse, Ruffian: THE LICORICE DAUGHTER: MY YEAR WITH RUFFIAN from TEXAS REVIEW PRESS. Other of Lifshin's recent prizewinning books include BEFORE IT'S LIGHT published winter 1999-2000 by Black Sparrow press, following their publication of COLD COMFORT in 1997.Other recently published books and chapbooks include: IN MIRRORS from Presa Press and UPSTATE: AN UNFINISHED STORY from Foot Hills and THE DAUGHTER I DON'T HAVE from Plan B Press. Other new books include WHEN A CAT DIES, ANOTHER WOMAN'S STORY, BARBIE POEMS, SHE WAS FOUND TREADING WATER DEEP OUT IN THE OCEAN and MAD GIRL POEMS. A NEW FILM ABOUT A WOMAN IN LOVE WITH THE DEAD, came from March Street Press in 2003. She has published more than 120 books of poetry, including MARILYN MONROE and BLUE TATTOO. She won awards for her non fiction and edited 4 anthologies of women's writing including TANGLED VINES, ARIADNE'S THREAD and LIPS UNSEALED. Her poems have appeared in most literary and poetry magazines and she is the subject of an award winning documentary film, LYN LIFSHIN: NOT MADE OF GLASS, available from Women Make Movies. Her poem, "No More Apologizing" has been called "among the most impressive documents of the women's poetry movement," by Alicia Ostriker. An update to her Gale Research Projects Autobiographical series, On The Outside, Lips, Blues, Blue Lace, was published Spring 2003. WHAT MATTERS MOST and AUGUST WIND were recently published. TSUNAMI is forthcoming from BLUE UNICORN. JESUS CHRIST POEMS will be published by Hazmat Press. World Parade Press will publish POETS (MOSTLY) WHO HAVE TOUCHED ME, LIVING AND DEAD: ALL TRUE, ESPECIALLY THE LIES summer of 2006. Texas Review Press will publish BARBARO: BEYOND BROKENNESS in 2008 and World Parade Books just published DESIRE in 2008. And DRIFTING is just online. Red Hen will publish PERSEPHONE in 2008. Coatalism Press just published 92 Rapple Drive and Goose River Press will publish Nutley Pond. Finishing Line Press will publish LOST IN THE FOG. For interviews, photographs, more bio material, reviews, interviews, prose, samples of work and more, her web site is www.lynlifshin.com.

Ballet Terminology

Pointe shoes, also referred to as **toe shoes**, are a special type of shoe used by ballet dancers for Pointe work, the act of standing on the toes while performing the steps of ballet. They developed from the desire to appear weightless and sylph-like onstage and have evolved to allow extended periods of movement on the tips of the toes (*en pointe*). Pointe shoes are normally worn only by female dancers, though male dancers may wear them for certain roles, such as the ugly stepsisters in *Cinderella.*

Barre, as used in ballet terminology, refers to a handrail used during warm up exercises. The term more widely refers to the series of exercises themselves, and also to the part of class which is comprised of barre exercises.

Turnout (also **turn-out**) is a rotation of the leg which comes from the hips, causing the knee and foot to turn outward, away from the center of the body. This rotation allows for greater extension of the leg, especially when raising it to the side and rear. Turnout is essential to classical ballet technique and is the basis on which all ballet movement follows.

Tulle is a thin, netted, often stiffened, silk, nylon, or rayon fabric used in ballet costumes, evening dresses and veils.

www.ingramcontent.com/pod-product-compliance
Lightning Source LLC
Chambersburg PA
CBHW060557030426
42337CB00019B/3567